THEORETICAL PRESENCE

Previous Journal Publication

Very Large Array, *Central Avenue*, May 2006
Nothing Happens, *Central Avenue*, September 2006
A Performance, *Malpais*, 2014
Laughter, Persistence, Bourbon, and Some Time, *Malpais*, April 2013
The Crusher, *Malpais*, Spring 2014

THEORETICAL PRESENCE

Poems

PHILLIP BRITTENHAM

Cover Art: Jerry Gorman, Italian Series, #2

© 2025 by Phillip Brittenham
All Rights Reserved
No part of this book may be reproduced in any form or by any electronic or mechanical means including information storage and retrieval systems without permission in writing from the publisher, except by a reviewer who may quote brief passages in a review.

Sunstone books may be purchased for educational, business, or sales promotional use. For information please write: Special Markets Department, Sunstone Press, P.O. Box 2321, Santa Fe, New Mexico 87504-2321.
Printed on acid-free paper
∞
eBook: 978-1-61139-788-8

Library of Congress Cataloging-in-Publication Data

Names: Brittenham, Phillip W. author
Title: Theoretical presence : poems / Phillip Brittenham.
Description: Santa Fe, NM : Sunstone Press, [2025] | Summary: "Poems by a well-known Southwestern US writer and artist"-- Provided by publisher.
Identifiers: LCCN 2025052338 | ISBN 9781632937797 paperback | ISBN 9781611397888 epub
Subjects: LCGFT: Poetry
Classification: LCC PS3602.R53328 T47 2025 | DDC 811.6--dc23/eng/20251212
LC record available at https://lccn.loc.gov/2025052338

WWW.SUNSTONEPRESS.COM
SUNSTONE PRESS / POST OFFICE BOX 2321 / SANTA FE, NM 87504-2321 /USA
(505) 988-4418

Dedicated with affection to my wife, Marti.

CONTENTS

BLUE STEEL ~12
MEMORY ~13
MEANINGS ~14
THE DREAM OF THE DOG FLYING ~15
GREEN EYES ~16
FOG ~ 17
THE SANDIAS ~ 18
STRING THEORY ~ 19
LA VERDAD ~ 20
MUSTANGS AT ALMA ~ 22
LOVE: AN ANALYSIS ~ 23
INCOMPARABLE ~ 24
UNDERGROUND ~ 25
VERY LARGE ARRAY ~ 26
SPRING WINDS ~ 27
A LAST REPAST ~ 29
CUTOUTS ~ 30
COLD CRANKING ~ 31
NO VALIDATION ~ 32
RESERVATIONS ~ 33
MY OLD COYOTE SKIN COAT ~ 34
NOTHING HAPPENS ~ 35
PANDORA'S BOX ~ 36
A PERFORMANCE ~ 37
HOLDING HORSES IN THE RAIN ~ 38
ATHENA ~ 39
STAKED PLAINS ~ 40
TASTE ~ 41
LOOSELY TRANSLATED ~ 42
MATTERS OF FACT ~ 43
LUCKY LADY ~ 44
LESSONS OF LAKE COMO ~ 45

LOCAL HISTORY ~ 46
TRES PISTOLAS ~ 47
HEAT LIGHTNING ~ 48
SLIVER OF MOONLIGHT ~ 49
CHICAGO EVENING ~ 50
BOOKISH ~ 52
'TIS THE SEASON ~ 53
SUNLIGHT ON AKROTIRI ~ 54
MUSTANGS AT GOLDEN ~ 55
OVERNIGHT MURDERS ~ 56
LESSER PRAIRIE CHICKEN ~ 57
SCALED QUAIL ~ 58
HOT WORK ~ 59
CELESTIAL BODIES ~ 60
THE GOD OF THIS PLACE ~ 61
FUTILITY ~ 62
VUGS OF EMPTINESS ~ 63
WE DON'T SPEAK OF IT ~ 64
HOTEL DREAD ~ 65
A RELATIONSHIP IN OTHER WORDS ~ 66
ACRYLIC ~ 67
WHISTLING UP WILSHIRE ~ 68
COYOTES ARE IN ON IT ~ 69
OUR TOWN ~ 70
DROUGHT ~ 71
GLORIA ~ 72
A KINDNESS ~ 73
CAFÉ DREAD ~ 74
SKIN GARDEN ~ 75
LIFE AND CASUALTY ~ 76
STUDY IN GRAY ~ 77
WELCOMING INFINITY ~ 78
DIMENSIONS OF CHOICE ~ 80
ISLE OF CAPRI ~ 81
A FAREWELL ~ 82

THE NIGHT OF CARINGTON GRAY ~ 83
MY OLD SOUL ~ 85
ARTFUL POSES ~ 86
BETTER POEMS ~ 87
NATURAL BRIDGE ~ 88
PENDEJO AND BIRD ~ 90
A NEW OWL ~ 91
A CAUTION ~ 92
SIDE POCKETS ~ 93
LAUGHTER, PERSISTENCE, BOURBON, AND SOME TIME ~ 94
HAPPY HOUR ~ 95
ALL THE WORDS ~ 96
THROUGH THE WINDOW ~ 97
A BOX OF CATS ~ 98
COMPOSITION WITH YUCCA ~ 99
BLUE NIGHTGOWNS ~ 100
SECOND CHANCES ~ 101
THE NEW SCHOOL ~ 102
ONE NOTE ~ 103
MARCH HARE ~ 104
ROUTINE MONSTERS ~ 105
SPLENDID ~ 106
THE BURNING ROAD ~ 107
THE CRUSHER ~ 108
CLOSED VILLAGE ~ 109
PINK CHIFFON ~ 110
OUTER SPACE ~ 111
AUTOMATED READER ~ 112
SHOUT OUT ~ 113
NIGHT FISHING ~ 114
A CAT IN THE PARKING LOT OF TIME ~ 115
PEOPLE AND POEMS ~ 117
THE MINOTAUR ~ 118
WINDFALL PEACHES ~ 119
PETROGLYPH ~ 120

PREFACE

This collection brings together many of my poems. It is obvious that free verse is not entirely free, that is, not written with complete abandon (see the last lines of "String Theory" for my feelings on this process). The poems in this collection use many traditional or nontraditional elements when deemed necessary and natural to the work, or unnatural depending on the effect desired.

These poems are wide ranging geographically and drawn from various places I have experienced, but I consider myself first as a New Mexico writer, maybe a New Mexico writer in Europe, but a New Mexico writer nevertheless. New Mexico has most profoundly influenced my perspective. I have often had desert grit in my teeth from the Sahara, to West Texas, to New Mexico. Some poems, like "Cutouts," depict challenges of desert austerity, and the transforming aesthetics of an uplifting effect is acknowledged in poems such as "The Sandias." Some New Mexico sand is typically blown onto the doorstep of memory.

Poems of a mythologizing feel transform into different kinds of statement such as those for our dear god Futility or the strange appearance accompanying the ladies in "Splendid." In "Athena," the identifiable myth is set to other work as are other ancient tales referenced ironically.

Ultimately, poetry exists for your intellectual delectation and amusement. So on with it.

BLUE STEEL

The assassin of the morning inspects
A weapon cocked to an intention.
It is flawless in performance.
Blue steel of the metrics delivers
Pressure of a moment to a firing pin
That only touches an explosive pellet
Of a meaning nestled in a bronze case.
The assassin's secret is to disguise
A hit that delivers the final word.
The assassin's secret is to make
It look like the ordinary violence
Of just another day executing itself.
This is the roundness of the metaphor,
But let us dishevel it a bit, my sweet,
Although I never intend to hurt you
With different messages or meanings.
Now place the barrel in your mouth.
Stoke its balls with gentle fingers
Until you find the trigger that will
Make you complicit in your demise.

MEMORY

Light is the first revelation, how it gilded
A room paused after some speaking,
Words not recalled but disappointing,
Perhaps evil after a fashion, but low
Evil that we cultivate in daily doings.
Furniture stands out, a nubby fabric,
Green rug, perhaps a table. Sometimes
A new chair appears; a sofa changes epoch.
So it is that we lose ourselves in a memory,
Become a viewpoint and little else.
No one speaks of it there, its meaning,
But the message is Remember this time
So you never think the past too sweet.
Then there is the hallway taking shape,
A woman, words, "I will not see you again."
Faces are blurred, and the moment is acute.
Someone has realized that the past is pain
And that we lurch away on broken bones.
Though virtual strangers, we feel it together.
The scene is suffused with an unspeakable
Poignancy, a sense of loss beyond consoling.
The moment called for a perfunctory embrace.
But was there a brief embrace after all?
Was I so uncharacteristically generous?
One must beware the play of imagination
Among the paused alabasters so arranged,
Lest they now begin to dance to that baton.

MEANINGS

Much underlies the unthought
Of a passive perception received.
In the little space defined as focus,
Words overheard seem pregnant,
Filled with a longing to speak
But are ultimately mute, deformed
Close to garbled as sound, noise.
The distance between the sounds
And significance is just too great.
By turning them in the mind as if
they were something in the hands,
Words, pieces, must somehow join
Into insights built of possibilities
To even approach comprehension.
At last, pieces fit into a meaning.
I have not seen the dog, you say
To a redhaired tank top anxious
On the periphery of your vision.
Talk is cheap to the man of words,
One might even argue, worthless,
But its meanings are seldom easy.
Imagine if she had asked you,
Quick now, what is the nature of love?
Wouldn't your reply have been the same
In whatever difference of words?

THE DREAM OF THE DOG FLYING

In the dream, the dream
Whose idea still charms me,
The dog flies as on a trapeze
Impelled across open sky
By a sheer will of doing so.
An expression fills its face with
Something akin to smugness.
Its freedom and delight are
Drawn upon surfaces so defined.
Later I see a hawk deep in sky
And imagine that it is the dog
Riding thermals high overhead
With short legs neatly tucked
And lingering on a sweet breeze.
The closest approach to the dream
Is that lift made possible in mind
Through a flute hauntingly played.
Opening the eyes then would be
To plummet not just down but back,
Striking the ordinary like a stone.

GREEN EYES

"What?" is a creature that hums
And chortles with the wind.
It makes you search fruitlessly
Among names of small birds
That hide in breaths of snow
To define a mystery with a word
For the What that approaches
Into the warmth you nurture.
It is but the werewind that calls
So lonely from falling snow
To nibble now at your neck,
Around the soft second skin
Of a woolly warm cocoon and
Chill your blood to a shiver.
Tooth severe and to the heart,
It says, "But it's just a little prick,"
That possesses you for a time
When the wind is high and
Whistles itself into such tunes
As to close your green eyes so.

FOG

Fog fingers through trees
Thick in tones of bluish gray.
In obscurity is revelation.
It has always been that way
Searching for a coherence.

Sounds are much heightened,
Voices closer, more urgent.
This is life in passing clouds,
Drifting slowly by the eye
In ways unknown before fog.

Fog seeps in to take people
From the sharp edge of clarity
To be dispersed like morning mist
Upon the wet hillside, diffuse, and
Disoriented in the uncertain light
Of a revelatory difference that is
Scattered like drizzle everywhere
As it appears in certain poems.

THE SANDIAS

Attention fixes at sunset
Upon on the flat screen
Of a distant escarpment,
A gradually burning pink
Foretaste of ethereal beauty
That slips over cliffs and crags.
Sipping a cold old fashioned
Makes me wonder if I ever
Really sipped an old fashioned.
It must be a delightful drink
Because it sounds so…you know.
The truth is what one makes of it,
That is, it must be true to the parable,
What you need to communicate,
But maybe not to literal accuracy.
A frontier bullshitter once said
He always told the truth except
When he didn't, except when
It was one of his wild "windies"
That taint the value of his history.
Poetry, contrariwise, conveys truth,
Even when it is factually untrue.
Now the porch is starting to look
A little iffy, and I, too, start to fade,
Not looking quite so typically so.
But when that thing lights up pink
With that special vibrant shade
And then breaks you open with it,
That is what you need to know.

STRING THEORY

Dry, rolling hills surround a ghost town,
A shadow town mostly gone to memory.
Bricks were made here and sent to the world
Until the world told them not to bother.
The highway wandered off without them.
A museum held a trove of knickknacks,
Geegaws, and other souvenirs of time
That told ordinary stories of daily life.
Most mesmerizing in the history of
Obsessive-compulsive disorder or
Close to it was a huge ball of string
From before tape and plastic bags
When packages were wrapped in paper
And tied with twine in a kind of
Presentable and practical artistry.
In those days, string came to one
Without so much effort to find it.
It required great care and patience
To wind layers of overlapping roundness
To hold the piece tightly together
With greater and greater concentration
Approaching a critical mass that
Could have blown a mind to smithereens.
Meter or rhyme, or any other extraneous
Organizing principle, would only have
Loosened the intensity of outcomes,
Distracted, and added nothing but trouble.

Phillip Brittenham ~ 19

LA VERDAD

Strums of a guitar. A rough voice
Carries over campground scrub,
Hesitates, and then sweetens to sing
Spanish poetry of passion and devotion,
La verdad, the truth existing between lovers.
The voice is studied and perfect in anguish,
And slow guitar notes string it to memory.
Night's lonely lyrics settle close to heart,
La verdad, the truth of the moment.

The listener faces forward always.
He is not distracted by the sentimental,
But the perfume of piñon smoke
In a stone house by the mountains
Conjures nearness of the memory
That touches him again in its return,
For it has only strayed from his mind
And moves him now as if heard from afar.
La verdad, the truth that is memory.

Less than a minute of recollection passes
Of what might once have been an hour
As broken fragments of a man singing
In depths of night before a golden fire.
The compression only concentrates,
Conceals nothing that must be known.
La verdad, the essence of that time
That will still be as true as its moment
A thousand years after memory has died.

A woman distractedly slumps in a chair
Staring into a large window purpling
As evening touches the mountains,

And her face is half-hidden in shadow.
The man briefly hovers, then asks,
"Do you recall that wonderful night…?"
He wants her to tell it in her voice.
He wants to hear it strum again in mind,
La verdad, which lives in two places.

MUSTANGS AT ALMA

Mustangs explode into the sky,
Raise their own storms of dust
On a steep trail to the impossible.
It is that burst of color I love most,
All the shades of horse blending
Against white stone of the butte.
I work the commotion in mind
Until it is supple and almost ready,
But it never is and never will be
Rendered fully in words alone.
Something vital is missing in mind
That cannot be touched or explained
Beyond my subtlest intervention.
Lacking is the energy driving them,
The determination of the intention
That I cannot portray in the vision
Of what it means to be that free.
As though I could even ponder
Riding the back of their journey
Or find a place in their wildness!
As though words have anything
To say on the way of that rough trail,
And they do this again and again,
Needing me less each time I see it.

LOVE: AN ANALYSIS

I am no incipient lover at this point
Lost in the grand purposes of love,
More of a technician, I suppose,
Trying to maintain its complexities.
Looking back on the curious thing,
I remember this slow walking
With one beloved on a busy street,
Enclosed in sets of quotation marks,
And singly so, not subsumed even then,
But always sensible and rarely sloppy.
The sky was bluer than mere sky,
Indeed, as reported by poets, and
Air was spicy, green was fluorescent,
And all else never more annoying.
But it was so evanescent all in all
As we moved to love's later stages.
There was this day when we passed,
Not hand in hand but still aware of it,
A slouched adobe church in Santa Fe
As doors sprang open and the bride
Known from another town and time
Exited, followed by a man, giddy with love,
In a moment that they had made together
From all their other improbable futures.
Stunned, we watched them from the curb.
Our consolations flapped like old shoes
Tied to the bumper and ran away with them.

INCOMPARABLE

The loveliest flower on the hill
Is the only flower on the hill,
That is to say, incomparable,
So early as to be considered late
In the turning over of seasons.
A pasque flower begins its bloom
On the shady side of the trail
Among the rocks and thin dirt.
Language cannot constrain it
As it makes the most of its time.
From small beginnings, it builds
A fragile cup of opaque blue,
Encircling petals closed such
That eyes cannot force them open.
It sways upon a sliver of a stem
Against violent winds of spring,
But a breath hesitates lest it
Blow the delicate petals apart.
A grace of elegance and form,
It disappears in a short time
Without ever opening fully
To reveal its secret heart.
I wander afar after others,
Stalking the scandalous beauty
Like an obsessive paparazzo
Searching through the rocks
For these cheesecake shots like
Memory clicking after memory,
But there was only the one flower.
What can a person do in this situation
But think of kitchen chairs and glue,
And the endless guile of flowers too?

UNDERGROUND

Elevators dropping underground
Could hold dozens more travelers.
I thread gloomy concrete trails alone
Through white confectionary stone,
Marvel at how long nature needed
To make slippery veils, a throne,
How long nature needed to make
Words that describe the stone.
I ooh and ah when I am supposed to,
Though maybe it is somewhat dreary.
A vast lunchroom advertises emptiness,
Which really is what is on display.
We are too early in the season still.
I would love a fine hot dog right now
With all the accoutrements slathered on,
But I confront aluminum queues
Dividing space for thousands smaller.
Slab sided, we line up so naturally.
I wonder about our reluctant journeys
Through such refined complexity,
The pennies sweating in my hand.
But lo, lit small in the far distance,
Persephone, goddess in a white apron
With a perky paper cap of purest white,
Does her time in the cold underground.
She wanly smiles at me and fluoresces
Behind the long, shimmering counter
With the prospect of my great love
Nestled warmly in her buns.

Phillip Brittenham ~ 25

VERY LARGE ARRAY

She is a smallish mammal imperfectly residing
Upon a tiny planet greatly overpeopled
In a cockeyed Milky Way corner half-done
That is somehow upon a longish drive
Around the cosmos with all the purpose
Of an endless Sunday afternoon.
Her husband pants like an excited dog
Before the open window of space/time.
He reads numbers from giant teacups set
In the desert floor that point upward
To search out lost time in the universe
That appears in abstract photographs
As a wondrous velvet of royal blue
Draped across the hard mathematics
Of sterile delight to a certain mind.
Unperturbed by cold galactic motions,
She arises early on this sunny morning
For oolong upon the verandah alone
While house and garden are quiet,
Before his voice fills the still air
With news of more miracles found
In the fire of infinitely distant galaxies.
The orange roses have fallen open
Overnight with a fullness threatened
By the slightest breath of breeze.
As sweetness sweats out of them,
She pronounces them exquisite.

SPRING WINDS

This is how we do spring out here
Where white paint holds steeples up
While America falls in upon itself.
This wind is the ocean we swim in.

Something tries to catch a breath,
Takes mine instead, and fills my lungs
With its violence and vindictiveness.
Pinprick stars litter a moonless sky.
Angry wind transforms a long night
Into something brutal and fearsome,
Transforms me as well to the core.
My brain is all over the forlorn plains,
Prowling streets of fly-speck towns
To leer into the filthy windows
As every fat wife tosses abed
And prays for her child and life,
And, bud, this ain't the blowjob
That you were expecting either.

There are no survivors. No one
Leaves such a night unchanged.
Trailers tremble in apprehension
Where people measure fierce gusts
In units of terror times intensity.
I breathe the madness of storm;
The bitter syrup of its darkness
Chokes me as it hangs in my throat.
Its power rattles and shakes me
As an inchoate craziness uncoils
And wails into night's chaos that
So much is loose, nothing is tight,
And nothing will ever be right.

Phillip Brittenham

Taste the ice and grit on my breath.
Look at metal wings vainly flapping
And feel the give behind the dreams.
I am the essence of this black wind,
Blowing down everything set in life.

God save all the tiny towns tonight.
God save the anxious pooch that
I cross on the way to bed tonight.

A LAST REPAST

I wish I were more entertaining, but I'm not.
The old charm scabs over quickly these days.
A little irritation spices dismal moments,
Leaving ice and bitterness on the tongue.
I linger on chores left undone, little things
That take on a necessity calling me now.
No one comes to take dirty plates away,
And we sit with the mess of our making
In the aftermath of a frugal lunch together
That starves the hungry soul for sustenance.
My companion is deliberately contentious,
As though challenging me with an urgency
Unspoken of her disappointment and regret.
She lets me see her as drained and forlorn.
Was she not glorious, butterfly gold and black,
As mornings filled hearts with her generosity?
This debridement of a relationship pains me
Like clatter from that bunghole of a kitchen.
We stare at one another, but neither mentions
A small death spread upon the table, ungrieved,
A dirty rag doll laid out for her needling.
I don't want to touch it, but it might be me.
I give the thing a greasy pinch and cry, Ouch.
Oh, the disappointments she carries around!
And some of them do appear to resemble me.
I no longer seem to meet her high expectations
That express the better nature of humanity.
Well, these are heavy, heavy times for all of us.
Our relationship returns to the capacious purse
Of her forgetting, back into a deeper emptiness
That was hers before she invented the universe.

Phillip Brittenham ~ 29

CUTOUTS

Wind-blown desert litter commemorates
Yet another failure to arrive anywhere
Across the scree of cobble fingerlings,
Dry sand, and brush of arroyo bottoms.

Purple cutouts outline distant horizons.
Cutouts of people define nearer air.
Sometimes we move through moments;
Sometimes moments move through us,
A world of holograms, a translucency
Of no feeling more intense than that.
Sunglasses out here should sport
Anywhere-else lenses, focus on infinity,
Bear the tint of indifference.

How much sunshine does it take
To expose the negative anyway?

Chances of survival look only fair today
In the old Apachería of the human heart.
Some cattle are posed, already stunned
And branded with commodity stares.
They have their own beef with futility,
The grass imagined just beyond the wire.

Like a headache revving up,
Blue moods of the desert
Ache across frontal lobes.
At times, the desert is grace.
At other times, nothing happens,
But without the grace to see it.

COLD CRANKING

Cold frosts both breath and brain as I
Select an intention from jangles of keys.
An old pickup won't start these mornings.
Won't, won't, won't, and won't,
Whines and coughs, blows black smoke,
The rusty bone of tailpipe dirties the snow,
Sputters just enough to break a heart.

A shaky morning hand goes numb
Twisting a key against the small
Resistance of a deep disappointment.

I open the hood with its coffin lid groan.
Darkness hidden there overnight flies off
Into deep purples that ink the dawn sky.
Pungent oil stink, the carrion smell of motor,
Carries intimations of mechanical ruin.
I remove the carapace of the dead carb,
Give her a couple squirts of gas, and
Smack the starter silly with a wrench,
The familiar invocations of the stranded.

I cuss the world good, cuss the luck that
Has snake bitten my life. My breath
Storms over the dash in frozen clouds.
As I twist the key again, I ask myself,
"How can so much desire still fit
Into such a small hole anymore?
Come on, baby."

By these dances and prayers,
Hope is finally delivered, coughing,
And squealing pained and surprised
Into a new world with infant cries
Of a fan belt finally grabbing hold.

Phillip Brittenham

NO VALIDATION

Not just parking is not validated here.
I have appeared at a reading as a horror
For a writer grown stiff and old, gravel.
He cannot even feign some cordiality.
Did I perhaps pinch off all his flowers?
Sometimes we involve things we regret.
Sometimes our invitations open in Hell.
Like most writers, he speaks of money.
Why, he could upend any of these old gals
By their bony ankles and sneakered feet
And shake out fortunes onto the floor.
Perhaps, I will rattle my chains and scare
The old ladies and overactive children,
Or perhaps I will just watch the cook
Across a narrow street filled with cars
Through the perfect frame of a window.
A contrast of black skin to white livery,
He leans distractedly against the rail
Of a small balcony in the beige wall.
The smoke of his cigarette is delight.
It becomes the essence of its freedom,
Becomes an encompassing all, drifting,
Enchanting even as it kills us both but
Makes the afternoon barely tolerable.

RESERVATIONS

The novelist was puzzled that he was there.
He wondered what a roomful of dry experts
Expected of him, what superior knowledge
They required when it was what he knew
Of humanity that modeled his characters,
Not some detailed anthropological flummery
That would turn them into academic stereotypes,
Albeit appropriately dressed and ritually correct.
It is enough to say that the boss, my boss,
Was capable of such unlikely aberrations
When filling a room with the best thinkers.

The novelist puzzled it for a while,
And then we two walked through fields
To visit a native woman he knew.
She puzzled it too and came to nothing,
Except maybe he should be someplace else.
These accidents happen when science mixes
Where it has no business, and its hard facts
Are facts of nonequivalence in the realm
Of intuitive wisdom and creative gentility.
At least it would not be my problem.
I was already gone and, to ease off of it,
Invited ten people to dine at a great place
Where the writer could speak thoughtfully
To the interests of these scholars over wine,
And they could swap stories one for one.
Somehow it came together at that moment.
I told the accountant, "Wait until the boss
Sees the bill for this." She misread me, winked.
"Oh, he never will. Believe me, he never will."
But that was not what I had intended at all.
It would have been ugly, so ugly and so fine.

Phillip Brittenham ~ 33

MY OLD COYOTE SKIN COAT

My old coyote skin coat hangs neglected
Among piles of dusty garage sale stuff
Where I have discarded the perfumed lies,
The animal deceits, the smothered truths,
And the little tricks of the duplicitous heart
That I once wore in such derisive comfort.
With reassurances of the old coyote skin coat
Snuggling me deep into heat of my own desire,
I tipped my graying muzzle to the stars
To demand more illicit favors of the moon.

My god, the affronts to my god.
My heart hardens with forgiveness.

The coat now weighs me down.
I swelter in its plush inner heat.
Moth-eaten, it was never new.
I sidle up to a young man in shorts
Who is thinking between his fingers,
Can I wear this old coyote skin coat?
Do I have the awful soul for it?
I say, "Try it on, son. It fits everyone,
If that is what you would choose,
And the price is so reasonable
For a young man in the prime of life."

NOTHING HAPPENS

Drunken librarians have burned books
And beaten writers and publishers
Dead in the night-rimmed streets,
For the alabaster foo dogs of their faith
Have died of a long starvation.

One cries out to me:

All day the child sits,
Invested in the book,
And still Nothing happens.

All day the killing continues,
And still Nothing happens.

Purveyors of defective shit.

All year round books collect,
Given number and dusty place,
And still Nothing happens.

Where are the wings that lift?
Where are the words of light?
I give her a wink upskirt
Before she stabs out my eyes
Upon her black high heels.

Is it all vanity and big bling?
Where, she wails, oh where
Is our Book of the Dead?

Phillip Brittenham ~ 35

PANDORA'S BOX

Pandora's box tuned in
Five hundred channels
Of uninterrupted infotainment.

But colors that fell through it
Turned gray on the other side.

It had a striking chrome grille,
Flared fenders, power mirrors,
And multidimensional stereo.

It made people think that
They would go very fast.

The fabric was woven by hand
In an intricate floral design
Serged with golden thread.

Visitors were lost forever
In its complex pattern.

The box was built of flawless
Mitered oak, perfection couch,
With rails of shimmering brass.

A gentle chime built-in announced
Second comings to anyone who cared.

Pandora's box was open 24/7, free delivery,
With ninety days same as cash OAC.

A PERFORMANCE

She is not a creature of sun, but radiant,
With the whitest skin they have seen
Beneath spotlights frying the tiny stage.
She says, You listen up, you young men,
And pushes a cowboy hat down upon her bangs.
This is how it was. The old man told you this
In the way back when:

Boys, first you get a dog.
The dog does all the work.
That's all you need to live.
Just the dog and the sheep.
Then you take the sheep up high
Where the green is experimental,
Where the peeks drop off the bottom
Of the whether. Then you loaf along
Just as you were, inventing words.
Maybe you can fish; you can hunt.

That's how it was, she says, once,
Only once, once upon a time.
She smiles, her finger like a wand
In the air of an undefined direction.

And why would you ever leave?
Well, why would you ever ask?
Sillies. For the love of a woman.
They whistle and stamp their feet
For a woman's love, she says, love
Big enough to cover the hurts and
Bigger than the barren begging bowl
Of the Earth he placed before you.

Thank you, gentlemen.

Phillip Brittenham ~ 37

HOLDING HORSES IN THE RAIN

Raindrops play staccato on a tin roof.
Boys, she says with an indulgent smile
As they jostle on the wooden benches.
The truth is what you think you know
When you are thinking of something else,
And that is how we sell our little poems.
She has a mind of dark and sultry snakes,
While they hear distant sirens in the wind.

You can tell she thinks she's smart.
She speaks in boldfaced feelings,
Winks at them in informed italics.
Her hands run down her pallid arms,
They hoot. They pound benches
And stamp their boots on cement.
They cannot hear the single quotes
Inside double quotes of her ventriloquism
Where their hearts are answering back.

Now, gentlemen, she coos to them,
Feel inside the raindrops as they fall
The words suspended inside the rain,
Words that are your poem tonight.

They would have held the horses all night
While she dug these holes in the rain.

ATHENA

Burnished bronze shield,
Golden warrior's helmet
Studded red with garnets,
She rivals morning light.
Her eyes are the mighty soul
Of the blue celestial glow.
Her head sculpted of marble
Is distracted, looking elsewhere,
Certainly not towards you.
She dresses in sheets of gold.
It is our Athena, she of olive
And she of furtive owl,
The lethal goddess warring
On brave heroes impaled,
Graced upon her silver spear.
There is so much left to know
That only a goddess can answer,
But to ask her your questions,
You who would know everything,
You who would peer into her mystery,
Would surely be to go blind.

STAKED PLAINS

Passage into the Staked Plains
Begins with one thought, one terror,
One regret, or one resentment and
Transitions across aspects of mind
Realized in a different fate made
As the heart possesses its destiny.
It looks like sand and yellow grass
Multiplied to horizons of infinity.
Blazing blue sky presses on eyes.
Lizards perform angry pushups
As vultures collect loosely above,
Scoffing at the desperate victim
Who wants only to escape the trap
Of the mind he has carried here.
Countless boot prints circle back
Upon themselves as destination
Like a lifetime of self-deception.
Scouring winds bear accusations
Of a deep, personal introspection
And fling judgments into the face
Of anyone who is lost out here.
Softer feelings shrivel in recalling,
Devolve into various inadequacies,
Leaving things hard and dark instead.
This is how someone is lost forever,
Lost to himself and to the world
In ways that could only be imagined
Before wandering the Staked Plains.

TASTE

Taste is preference expressed
Among aesthetic decisions
For reasons good and bad.
It is what it is, a complex tale
Told by the senses and censored
By personal predilections.
This was illustrated well when
A biker friend fell in love with
A profoundly vapid woman.
Taste may be emotionally
Deformed by derangements
Of this kind, and by others,
But love is a familiar suspect.
Her features were severe
To the rational observer,
Her voice an annoying cackle.
He reported that he daily
Spent hours just savoring
The rich tang of her beauty
Determined and appraised
With great satisfaction
In the inebriated dimness
Of a doublewide trailer,
Just looking thereupon.

LOOSELY TRANSLATED

It is bad moment for both of us.

By a rock, by a juniper root,
In cool sheltering shade,
Ominous rattling intrudes
Loosely translated into air
Of a rocky morning trail.
An abhorrence, a loathing, and
A visible repugnance recoil
To elude the abrupt revelation
That is the desecration here.
The fault is entirely mine.
Attention levels peg.

Of a wholly different passage, it says:
My thoughts are not your thoughts,
And your ways are not my ways, pal.
This is how it is at the meeting
As rattles affirm the warning,
Dangerous words of an older text
Recalled in this moment between us,
And still I find them striking.

Although we all look different in books.

MATTERS OF FACT

Curiosity is the norm in science,
But when that snake-charmed wild
Naked woman entices you with
An unimaginable fruit forbidden with
Unseen consequences beneath its skin,
Do not play the fool and just eat of it.
Rather document its habits, its forms,
Its chemistry, and its propagation.
Rename it not as bald disobedience
But as science of a providential nature
With its always theoretical roundness
Lingering so enticingly in the intellect.
Savor it artistically, too, in its place,
In the still life that forms about it
Where it can only be imagined
To taste as sweetly complex as
The rich layering of various evils
That we already know so well.

LUCKY LADY

O lucky lady. O wonder woman.
I am interested in your pockets,
Equally both front and back.
First there is a wallet to dine upon.
Waiters perplexed by pidgin Italian
Tell us that everything is impossible,
But what do they know of this us?
We speak so many languages poorly,
But our meanings are mutually true!
There is this deeper darkness too
That hides in depths of pockets.
We live in such shadows as these,
We who live alone in mysteries.
Rings of keys, rings of possibilities,
Are the great symbols of your magic,
Your exquisite power in the world.
Maybe a key clicks in the heavy door
Of space-time, as in a fine automobile,
Or a door lock to some loft room
Not too far from the Grand Canal.
Perhaps some coins and wadded bills
Can purchase a fine compass in a shop
To tell us where we are yet to arrive,
The convergence to our true north.
At the warm bottom of everything,
A lovely piece waits to be exalted
For our entertainment and delight,
A blessing upon our new friendship.
Forget the page of reservations,
The carefully crafted commitments
Folded and refolded into a back pocket
As something complex and irrevocable, for
We will rewrite the meaning of forever
To define our little time together here.

LESSONS OF LAKE COMO

It is not a true window cut
To shores of lovely Como,
But only printed cardboard
That is learning the Italian
I hear spoken in my heart
In a musty basement room.
Daily I tutor the photograph.
Color by color, word by word,
The thin lines and outlines
Downshift into deeper shadows,
Accelerate into complexities.
The flat, printed sky speaks
With newfound confidence
Of a much deeper, older blue,
Applied with palette knife and
Smeared in thick undulations.
The foreground is learning
To whisper deceitfully to me,
To layer its browns and yellows
With all the colors underlying.
Plants of sinuous purple and black
Are written cryptically on the shore
That once was empty and mute.
Along a reddish turn of dirt road,
Stucco walls define angles of light.
Where some gray once blended,
Blocks of pure color now contrast
Down to the water, to the beach,
And the resurgent susurration
Of the gentlest waves trilling
Their blue, green, and white
Onto the newly instructed sand.

Phillip Brittenham ~ 45

LOCAL HISTORY

Newspapers overlooked the day
I crossed the flat, juniper dustlands
And climbed to reach the mesa top
That was our version of a peak.
Someone unseen took a shot in the brush;
Cows looked away in total innocence.
The sun assumed a Western quality
As I sweated up the hill to the flat place
Where a person could see all the world
In an amber refinery haze. I counted
Coup on the universe of wild desires.
I slapped my own back theoretically,
Then returned to life largely unchanged
For the grandeur of the conception.
Memories were briefly savored and
Eventually formed into this poem
Where the incidents, once fresh, die
Hanging with these hard characters.

TRES PISTOLAS

A poem failed along this mountain trail,
Stumbled on the hard, dry elements
Of sky, sun, and rock that would
Not be moved to any useful meaning.
Solace that day was whatever shade
Lingered on the other side of boulders.
Here is where fingers slid around stones
For some significance, and dry sand
Held no words deep down to answer.
And here gray birds flew away surprised
In a burst, denying their participation.
The sun, at the very top of its game,
Still refuses comment for notation
As I follow the trail down the same way,
Crippled on crumbled granite underfoot,
I grieve the dearth of poetry not harbored
In confines of a sterile environment
Manifested along the wandering trail
Where I am always the central point
Of moods that coincide into landscape
Or slip into the brush of disappointment.

HEAT LIGHTNING

Sun sets in pink pizzazz.
Heat lightning sparks,
But heat does not lessen.
The dog has followed his nose
And is on the town tonight
To some trash cans he knows.

A woman's voice fades on the wind
As she plaintively calls his name
Again and again into the darkness,
The tone promising eternal love,
Unrestrained loyalty, snuggling,
And unconditional forgiveness,
If he will only return to her.

I hold an empty collar full of envy
On a dark corner he will likely pass.
Buffeted by droplets of rain in the face,
I wait for the disobedient hound
To bolt from the shadows around me,
Arrogant and dismissive in his freedom.
My dear, the dog is not the only one lost
In the wild storm tonight and waiting
For your voice to call him back.

SLIVER OF MOONLIGHT

Someone will die tonight,
Cut on a cat's eye sliver
Of ugly orange moon,
A twilight world revealed.
Tree leaves tremble on an
Anxious breath of wind, and
An expectancy sparks in the air
That something is wrong tonight.
That something craves a death
To reset its precarious balance.
These few boys bronzed on bikes
Gathered beneath the street lights
And laughing through their smokes
As if unaware, as if they don't see it,
Won't be laughing for long,
When someone dies tonight:
Face up, alone on the dirty street,
In a pool of night's revelation,
With a sliver of moonlight
Embedded in his eye.

Phillip Brittenham ~ 49

CHICAGO EVENING

Cool lake breezes push heat aside,
And leaves shake urgently beneath
The gray matte of gathering clouds.
Young women collect on platforms,
Massive arms of painted airborne iron
Holding up shade to streets below.
They chat freely of common friends,
As gray pigeons flutter by, unnoticed,
And there is a little freedom in the air
Now that work is done and evening
Approaches in sprays of long light
Across the rippling surface of the lake.

Trains squeal across old Chicago,
And heavy-lidded riders rest content
To sway gently into a necessary journey
That they count as so much wasted time.
Women arrange coats, purses, and
Packages into too little space.
A few men bristle alert, watching,
Waiting for something to happen,
Defying any useless human contact.
Kids, boisterous, black, confident,
Celebrate their comradeship.

Dollops of warm rain drip onto windows,
Smearing hard geometry of brick buildings
To something finer, and summer colors
Blur into collages of everyman at ease.
Proximity invites gaze into kitchens
Stirring with good stuff on the stove.
Evening snapshots of urban artifacts collect,
And no one knows that they are in them,

In some casual community of composition.
And if they did, would they turn for a moment,
Turn for just a moment on their weary way,
And smile for me, smile for me as if posed for me?

BOOKISH

At last, I find the one book for you
Among dusty boxes and shelves
Of all that I am losing with a will,
But first there was the book of you
That I had to read and understand
To give a book that is you in all regards,
Whimsy surely, nothing serious or sad,
Funny, oh god yes, nothing too strenuous,
Nothing too modern, something quaint.
Don't look a book horse in the mouth,
I guess we would say for the occasion,
But do judge us by our ragged covers
Or at least what they used to be.

Something old in a cloth of blue will do
That I have never much loved for myself,
That I kept because it delighted in its touch,
The thick skin of pages that do not bend
Where a publisher made a big book of a story.
It is one that charms and is not tedious.
This is the one I have saved that you can enjoy,
A theoretical presence finding its way to you.

'TIS THE SEASON

For lyric poets at imaginary work,
'Tis out by two and, Good day,
Mrs. Huddleston. Don't forget
To bury the terrible stollen deep.
Only casual browsers shopping
For a housewarming poem today.
Romantic verse is usually
In high demand, but not now
With holidays so close upon us
And shopping to ease the heart.
Maybe a foot-warming poem
Will move to that right person,
The one I often think of now.
It is hard to put two nickels
Together with such rhymes,
But bless that broken woman
With the lightful elfin ease,
Recumbent of the current season.
No sense her dragging that cast
On empty streets, clacking along
When the poem can come to her.
Clock arms go empty but noticed.
She said she would just veg in bed,
And I too may favor a leg today.

SUNLIGHT ON AKROTIRI

Imagine quiet beauty of a village
In remarkable seaside sunlight
Over beach and ocean and plains.
The lithe beauty of people drapes
In grace as they fish and work
In remarkable frescos left.
Then a volcano blows up the world.

Lights switch on and shaped stones
Live incandescently without souls.
Someone interrupts to ask the guide,
"Where did they go after the disaster."
"They are still here," she says, "Out here,
Huddled on plains above the shore.
Someday we will find them there."
I don't think they will, immured in stone,
As distant now as modern neighbors.
It is painful to worship the artifacts,
To dream in a past present in the form
Of lavish idyll that touches feelings.
When we dare to confront the images,
We watch the children of calamity,
Dying, but from our perspective.

MUSTANGS AT GOLDEN

A small band of five,
They are not wild horses
Climbing these volcanic hills
And moving along in grass,
At least not in official jargon.
Despite the late correction,
These horses do look wild,
Untouched, and independent
In their vocabulary of motion,
But one who speaks the language
Says that wild has been removed
From their kind of autonomy.
Now called managed horses,
They are counted, assessed,
Recorded, and diminished
Wherever such tallies reside
Far outside the imagination.
It is a word only for managers.
Wild is what these horses live
In the fullness of its meaning
And in the freedom we see
As we watch them wander.
A managed horse is surely
Something else entirely,
Much like married persons,
Who so tamely reside
Inside strictures of words.

OVERNIGHT MURDERS

First snow blew in late last night,
An unexpected storm swept on words
Of chagrin and regret at changing seasons.
Words noticed a difference in the sky
And ferocious gusts from the south,
But evidence melted to gloss by morning.

The wrecked garden reveals
Vandalism left by night wind
That broke geraniums over and
Discloses the quick work
Of the deadly winter cold
That murdered to the root.
A cloudless sky of bastard blue
Professes ignorance of the deeds
Like a shielding smile.

Words linger on the scene, resigned,
And do not disguise the fate of flowers.
Indifferent breezes sweep the whole affair
Into musty mats of leaves beneath barren trees
Where remains of summers reside, unspoken
While killers go freely about their work.

LESSER PRAIRIE CHICKEN

A fanciful oddity is
The lesser prairie chicken
That is the litigated
Lesser chicken overall
Than the greater one.
It ranges endangered
Throughout the sage and
Dismal, undifferentiated
Backhand of the West,
Blooming with warbles,
Pursed of bright colors
That blend nevertheless
And also everthemore
Into the great dun Blah,
Which scarcely sustains it.
And what do they do
To merit preservation
(As some would ask of us)?
Beauty itself is an answer.
But know that they do
Lesser prairie chicken forth,
Regardless of our judgment,
Clucks to the last.

Phillip Brittenham

SCALED QUAIL

Maybe just scaled
To expectations of a quail
Feathered like chain mail,
It peeps and pops from brush
Eloquent in its aplomb,
Unperturbed and uncurbed
In the dire scrub wastes.

This scaled quail would walk
Rather than flip a wing
Into the soft blue down
Of a precarious sky.
Mostly invisible, it hides
In the field of our blindness
Where complexity resides.

Possessive or contracted,
Grammatically uncommitted,
Its head sports an apostrophe
Or a thought balloon perhaps
That is a space for afterthoughts
Such as this oddity:
Also called blue quail,
It is gray where we find it.

HOT WORK

Blowing glass is hot work in hot country.
Glass emerges molten orange from
A hellish furnace, and a creator's breath
Bequeaths a form to the formless mass,
Expanding a globule to the very size
Of a vision from which it is finished.
Later it is resting on a shelf with others,
Filled with emptiness, pellucid but muted,
Perhaps waiting to be filled with juice.
Light has gone out inside its structure.
But eventually, it fills with light of sunset
Until the star is reflected and echoed
Across its perfect sheen and roundness
Where we also see ourselves skimmed
Beneath the rim of its lively apparitions
As it glows again with fire of an artistry.
At last, we see it for the vessel it is that
Will deliver us to these visual wonders
Revealing a minute, intricate beauty and
Transforming it in the tilt of the glass
That makes art of the world around us.
We see how fragile it is, how unsuited
It is to linger thus with us in this world
Of accidents and other like disturbances
Affecting our modes of transportation.

Phillip Brittenham ~ 59

CELESTIAL BODIES

The speckled kingsnake
Was never seen here before.
It was ebony with an appliqué
Of golden speckles dappled
Down its black length like
Night sky mapped until one
Thought of stars, not snakes
As it spoke of deep space.
It will not be seen again,
But it remains in memory,
Which only dims the vibrant
Experience of the natural.
Glossy snakes, also beautiful,
Carry pastel shades of the land,
But this snake was different.
Air around it filled with new-made
Myth and wonder for a reptile surely
Touched by the generous hands
Of old gods of this world who hid
The gold of their greatest work
Underground or beneath stones.

THE GOD OF THIS PLACE

O Traveler, beware in this dry land
The god of this place, Futility,
Deity of small, cracked stones
And flinty caprock ridges
Where no grass ever grows.
The scowl is his, unkind words,
Mutterings that steal faith away,
Dry spit, and midnight cry.
The thorn is his emblem
And the hard, ingrown knot
Of the juniper that wraps
Black arms around the soul.
The grackle names him
Lord of the raggedy poem,
The exceptions fallen from
Apollo's sweet, hypnotic lyre.
Dry thunder shakes his realm.
He is immortal in his yearning
And worshipped only by those
Most predisposed to worshipping.
You may sacrifice to him, if you will,
Offerings of fat, burned meat
And sweet, strong drink and song,
Or not, since he is powerless
And has no gifts to give you.

Phillip Brittenham ~ 61

FUTILITY

I cannot wishbone their many lacks away.

Oh, how we do go on! They bring great feasts
Of most succulent meats to burn before me.
They bring the finest wine and pour it out
Upon the ground to please this god, this me,
Though I would suck sweetness from the earth
And richness and fat from the black char
For but a momentary taste of what is real.

So it is that I dandle grace before them,
But never let them actually enjoy it.
I burn their dreams to smoke and emptiness
Until they are no longer habitable by men.
Is it any wonder we have developed bad attitudes?

They ask questions about the future, what comes,
I answer that it too is only a hollow thing, a void,
But they vex the very air to frenzy about it.

So it is.
We owe each other, but we don't know what.

Even gods pass away, pass into a death
If not something else, like a whirlwind
Tearing itself into invisibility. I am weary.
I am weary of the drone of voices pleading
As if I am the author of this place. Behold
The god Futility and his people, the Mediocrities.

VUGS OF EMPTINESS

Along the trail down, in an unsure place,
A young man removes a stone fallen in his way,
And there is no underside, only a blackness
Reaching deep into the ground, the end unseen.
His face blanks with the ardor of doubt.
The Devil might say, That's quite funny
When faith falls away like that, my friend!
Maybe God would say, There were only seven days,
You see, and so much to be done and not every
Top got a bottom, like that lightless plummet
In your soul deep into the vugs of emptiness.
A prospector who knows the complexities
And voids holding up his surfaces, though,
Warns him in the inevitable voice of a priest,
I'd surely step away, son. Step away lightly.

Phillip Brittenham ~ 63

WE DON'T SPEAK OF IT

We won't discuss the snow
Or the sizzle of kernels of ice
Puddling upon the woodstove
As a screenful of white static
Replaces the known world.

We won't speak of the terrors
Of driving, the strange free
Dance of automobiles on ice,
Or the eventual loss of faith
When one is stuck a long time
In a lot of ways and realizes it.
We won't linger on the stories
Of couples snowed in so long
They had no choice but to part,
Knowing what they know now,
Tender feelings blasted from disuse
As they emerged wordless from storms.

Isolation, separation, deprivation,
The -shun words lurch about
Through winters lost in the heart—
When the breath transubstantiates
Itself briefly into the visible realm
Like the things we should have said,
And a blunt, rusty shovel strains
Against the heft of the weather
Like the unbearable weight of things
In which we no longer believe.

HOTEL DREAD

In the caul of a seamless night,
Sounds are readily confounded
And amplified in a hotel hallway.

He waits like a panhandler barricaded in an alley
Of darkness and indecision of his own making.
He has articulated a small space between boxes
From the neighborhood of a deep emptiness
With his liquor bottles, excesses, and books.
So the days go by without a penny for the old guy
Until he knows how it feels to be this alone,
A plucked chicken, the semblance of a man,
Face red and puckered with regret, refuted thus.

He shouts out to the sound of rescuers.
I am here. I am still here, gentlemen.
Look for me by the cardboard boxes,
But it is only some lost dogs at it again,
Lost dogs in the street having their say,
Or voices of travelers in the hallway,
Barking their complaints to management.

Phillip Brittenham ~ 65

A RELATIONSHIP IN OTHER WORDS

As for the betrayal, or noticeable absence,
Left by a woman of a kind walking away
Or, more accurately, sneaking out and
Entering into the fact of an abandonment
From a truly idyllic domestic situation,
Or make that, rather, a necessary recovery
From the aphasia of a long embrace
That was maybe more like a headlock
In the stark anteroom of a certain hell,
Be assured that no one ever foresaw it,
No one but one anyway, that one,
The one that was once so cherished,
That is to say, was always so overlooked.
Another woman, also of a kind, then feels
The magnetism, the pull, no, the force,
Or, more precisely put, the suck
Of an unexpectedly available vacuity.

ACRYLIC

When Billy fired
From the jailhouse stairs,
A slug gouged the wall
Deep into the adobe.
This is the story we tell,
Though truth rode away
With legendary tales
Of Billy's renown.

Enlarged by every boy's
Finger and imagination,
The hole was covered
With an acrylic sheet,
Like the ones placed
Around a foam sculpture
Of a woman's breast
That read Please Touch,
Temporarily on loan
From a Paris gallery.
The soft touch of truth
Was denied before
The hard plastic of time.

Noli me tangere,
Said Jesus Christ,
On loan to the world.
Make of the theology
What acrylic you will.

WHISTLING UP WILSHIRE

By seven on a sunny LA morning,
Warm animal scents start working
From the worn blanket and sheets
On the rock-hard motel mattress.
Acrid, almost angry, these smells,
These spirits warmed back to life,
Speak again of their old passion,
Meat on meat, the rich stew of life,
Husband and oily wife conjoined.
So familiar music plays in the mind,
Not dainty, just restless and necessary.
When mankind asks about its origins,
Tell them it was in a motel on Wilshire.
When mankind asks why it exists,
Tell them it is because there was time
On a long Sunday morning. And so
We go on with our own purposes,
Whistling carelessly up Wilshire
Past sooty stones of buildings,
Past tar pits and stinks that bind us.

COYOTES ARE IN ON IT

The persistent fretwork of wind
Blows late winter wool over hills,
Chills our high tops, and retints the land.
Coyotes, inspectors of change, are working,
Yips echoing behind every ridge, nosy
For all the difference they would know.
And they are in on it, whatever's changed.

Morning sunlight reflects off the dawn face
Of mountains and riddles snowbanks
Until only a lace of crystals sustains them,
A fragility that could collapse on a breath.
Thus penciled edits hollow morning's poem
Beneath a surface that stands just on a word,
Ready to implode into a painful incoherence.

Resting on your breast is such a moment too,
For nothing holds up the experience—
A night alone in the frozen wilderness.
Then I am strangely gone in a moment,
Distressingly superficial for all I said
As the poem dripped down the page.
I melt carelessly back into sunlight,
And the coyotes are surely in on it.

OUR TOWN

Old men all over our little town
Wildly dance in attic windows,
Spinning and bumping themselves
Delightedly against wooden frames
In some most disturbing ways.
Of course, we blame the poetry.
One demented man dances naked
In a plum purple house downtown,
Wagging his ancient junk about
Lasciviously for all to see.
Concerned residents warn us
That we could become known
For this, if for nothing more.
A motion is thus being placed
Before this august council
To allow the sale of poetry
To the young who need its news
But to withhold it from old men
Who have nothing better to do
Than to jounce in window frames,
Dancing with the freedom of kings.

DROUGHT

Arrives the day to a dry stretch
Where even timeless yucca says,
Time's up. The durable piñon
Dies in a shower of brown needles,
Leaving its outstretched arms
Stark against a cloudless sky.
Wind throws fireballs around you
As you stumble across a brittle land
And emit soft fragrances of flowers.
A rattlesnake unwinding in some shade
Thinks, We see so few angels now.
Now that rains have stopped for good.
He reads your little love in heat you emit.
Your pink sneakers move like small rabbits
Here where even rabbits have moved on.
The distress is all around you, but you
Cannot feel it, feeling nothing but free.
Self-contained, you sway and you slosh
With various liquids of your enchantment,
Vodka, vermouth, love and giggles,
Blind upon dead sand, festive, my dear.

GLORIA

When Gloria enameled her desk
One gray afternoon in 1962
With crayons and a curlicue,
Red ink and hosannas,
Pencils and blue markers,
Around the ordinary name
Of that thug with the Elvis hair,
A realization reached my heart
That she had not cared for me.

For an hour, she had sat there
Inking that name into the wood
And apotheosizing him in school,
Knowing what she must do
And what would happen later,
Powerless to stop herself.

No one recognized it then,
What spilled out across her desk
Willful, wild, and personally true.
When she cursed the angry teacher
And jumped right out the window,
No one knew then to run after her
Into the advent of a defiant new art.

A KINDNESS

On the splintered stoop
Of a house melting
Back into red dirt,
A woman made old
By winters and wind
Stirs the soft earth
With a crooked stick
As she sits quietly
In a box of sunlight
Framing the moment.
Vestiges of a breeze,
Neither warm nor cold,
Play smoothly across
Lapsed conversation.

She mutters after a time,
With fragile weariness,
I guess I will have to
Rip out that tangle
Of bindweed woven
Into the garden now.
She shakes her head
And adds in a voice
That holds her seasons,
It all started in January
With a kindness, I suppose,
When I put out some seed
For the winter birds.
And that is just how
It has been with love.

CAFÉ DREAD

Only the freshest ingredients would do
At the magnificent Café Dread that night.
Hot grease sizzled and hissed all round.
Flames casting wispy shadows on walls
Danced in dim light of a crowded room.
Hope you like it rare, the chef cried,
Swinging silver cleavers over his head
Until they sparked in the smoky air.
Beef, fish, and lamb filled platters.
Starving waiters, expressions speaking
Want in Third World dialects, watched
And drooled over the garlic snails
Incinerated in their blind shells
To be sucked into a fat man's gullet.
Where is justice now? waiters cried,
Broken by weight of their service.
The pâté was bleeding succulently
When Abdullah, the would-be prophet,
Suddenly switched on all the lights.
Even the bold Abdullah was astonished
At the empty room of his dream of hunger.

SKIN GARDEN

A skin garden of nasty stinks
Washes away in lucious aromas
Pronounced as flower names.
For us, frothy jasmine bubbles
Of goat milk soap from the far hills
Scrub a deeper clean. Our hands,
Our filthy parts, our special places,
Glisten inside goat milk soap bubbles.

The dog briefly noses in, unamused,
Puzzled by the frivolity expressed
In such loud bursts through the house.
So it yawns towards a long afternoon
Of laughter and sighs together in the tub
Thus reposed deliquescent and splish
Splashing in cool water like children
With this very notion of a lasting clean
Down to the rainbow skim of old soul,
Purified at last and awaiting the touch
Of just anything to dirty itself again.

LIFE AND CASUALTY

This spicy pulsing in the blood
Is like the decisive crunch of wicker
When someone is finally getting up,
The crack of bones beginning to move.
The road honey gal who steers me
Once prophesied we would return here
To the piquant heat of the desert
Where the chile strains converge.
So I have resumed my career, you see,
Of gingerbread man with a sugared soul,
Hot cinnamon eyes, and a pinch of cayenne.
I ring the bell of a coldly cultivated inner air,
Dong, Dong, for so it resounds throughout
A big and useless house of so little living.
I get a smile and a foot in the massive door
And disclose cases of oddments and curiosities
Tinged with the aroma of anise and molasses,
The smell of soulful curries waking up,
Chipotle, peppercorns, and Hatch green chile
Filling the rooms with the slow, even burn
That we in the business call life assurance.

STUDY IN GRAY

The gray bulk of elephants and hippos
Swells a room in twilight before dawn.
A gorilla vaguely formed darkens a wall
As anacondas twine around their shadows.
Disguised as a set of soft-sided luggage,
I am hidden beneath a dim leaf of light
Emitted from the little lamp on the table.
Manatees float just below the surface
Of liquid darkness rippling around me
When their noses touch the surface.
I wait hungry in stillness of the room
Over the indictment of an empty page,
Gripping the cold shaft of a pen and
Hoping to spear something smaller,
Hoping for a quick kill on the point
With the warm taste of fresh blood
As I cut an artery of something vital.
All is gray and indistinct in my lair,
Where necessary clarity never appears.
Sometimes it feels as though my head
Has shrunk to the size of a baseball
With skin sere as dried tobacco leaf
Stretched across the memory of a wail.
It swings on a thong before a lodge
Where tourists say it looks almost real.
Old men of the forest explain to them,
"He was a mighty hunter in the jungle
But became indifferent to other creatures
In his way and so starved to death
In complications of the understory."

Phillip Brittenham ~ 77

WELCOMING INFINITY

With what mask of true face
Dare we welcome infinity,
Even if it is only such infinity
As we can comfortably conceive?
Noon sun scarcely penetrates
Depths of shadow and stone.
A net sifts disturbed air below
For those who would fly
With futile human motions
From railings of the bridge.
Visitants lean over the edge,
But never as far as imagined
To actually fall into something.
Cheap thrills are obtained here.
They must stand a while alone
As if viewing a painting of the same,
Including an audience in its design
Before realizing that one could soar
On thin wings of the hawklike
Fearlessly along volcanic walls,
Consuming stark gifts of time,
The grandeur, and eroded contours.
But such freedom can also imperil
A casual soul vacationing here
As gravity grabs hold and fliers
Dangerously descend deep below
The scale of self to confront
What assumes a shape in mind
Of a devilish vision of stone teeth
In the maw of lethal desolation.
Wings of wax and sticks flutter
On the harsh breath of the sublime,
An awful shudder that transpires

At the moment of its appearance
Before the final uplift ensues,
Tempered with magnificence.
They walk away, shaken.

DIMENSIONS OF CHOICE

A lifeline is here, then disappears,
Around a soggy choice in Venice.
Three steps from the green door
In Florence, I cannot find myself,
No matter where I left it behind.
Only kind strangers can save me
If I can read their gesticulations,
Pursed lips, and grim headshakes
That say "impossible" so well.
They would have me turn to dust
And just blow away if I could
Since my situation is impossible.

In a room of doors in Versailles,
The guard says I can go anywhere
In this shrine of lavish freedoms
But not there or here, not this door
Or that, whichever I would choose.
The little man will not let me lose
By opening the wrong anywhere.
I long to plant him in the petunias,
But I should thank him, I suppose,
For teaching me to think in French,
For exposing the futility of choice,
Which never opens where it should.

ISLE OF CAPRI

How often when I am trapped
Dispirited inside the moment,
I return to the sight of Capri
Through a pinhole in time
That was only a small porthole
Deep in the middle of night
While the ship trembled beneath.
It was such a remarkable place
That my mother wakened me
With excited whispers to see it.
Not glittering and not brilliant,
Only the cold blankness of night
Reflected back from the glass
While imprinting on the mind.
With each recollection, I travel
Deeper into a blackness glimpsed
That can never be lit by sunlight,
That can never be anything else
More meaningful than its memory.
I could have gone to Capri later,
But nothing resided there for me
Wandering the beaches glumly,
Lost in my Speedos and flip-flops
As if confused by something else.

A FAREWELL

These new cuts into the forest
Perturb the creek-side solemnity
Of shade stiffly brewed through
Canopies of leaves and sunlight.
These cuts disturb the loneliness
Where it finds itself in distance.
A trailer erases remoteness forever.
How I loved these woods, losing
Myself ten yards from the road
With a sense I penetrated too far,
But I was always near the road.
With these intrusions, the savoring
Of the experience has changed.

I wore a particular lumberjack shirt,
Always dressing for the part but
Not packing the requisite gear. A real
Lumberjack said that maybe it was not
The lumberjack shirt, that it was only
The shirt sold in the store in the town.
Love charts in lines of ups and downs,
Of floating medians always in flux.
My love has matured with knowledge.
It has changed as the forest changes
And as the seashore is betrayed
By development and rewriting storms.
I have attained some closure at last.
I have been seeing other mountains,
Wading other waters, but I will miss
The lost integrity of a damaged place
As a wound that haunts my heart.

THE NIGHT OF CARINGTON GRAY

Calmness of mind meets night stillness.
This moment is for the pobres who
Cannot write the dream or find where
Their thoughts are drawn into it.
Which one of us will not play the part
Of an unrealized person pillowed and
Drawn towards sleep on edge of insight?
Or alternatively mind moves so fast
It stands still as it notices everything
Speeding around and through it.
Darkness transitions into difference,
Hanging its thick honey nightwise.
Let me explain how the dead air is
Drawn into lungs of shallow breathing
Forming free verse mumbles on the lips.
A blanket of coolness lies over the bed
Where time slows and a thoughtful scratch
Takes eons of dinosaur time. The body is
An itchy thing of many complications
As it lies abed, haunted by its needs.
Reality, dissected and savored piecemeal,
Is compromised with other conditions.
Paintings are passages into walls as though
One could pass inside the invitation.
No substance appears but tones of gray
Shaded with blunt ends of the chalk,
Anonymous until named Carington Gray,
Obliterating the smooth grayscale of infinity
With this particularity. Very classy.
It is the first kiss of dawn upon the last sigh
Of darkness. It is disclosure and secrecy,
An in between that repaints the canvas
With different understandings and patience

In blocks of Carington Gray and at last
Recalls the return of what is only expected.
As it is not the color, it is not the night
That plays in mind, but its resonance.

MY OLD SOUL

Cops picked up my old soul last night
Huffing down a lonely boulevard,
Past temptation, drunk and disorderly,
In search of rap, jazz, rhythm and blues,
The soft and easy skin of the night
As wicked women swoon with dance.
They would have returned it sooner,
But they said it had no fingerprints,
No characteristics, no identity,
And it had disavowed me again.

It slurred its words and pounded
A giddy beat into the furniture.
The shrill reed of a saxophone,
It explained when the cops left
With just a warning to the wise,
Had made it weep and dance
And burned its face with happiness
Such that it no longer would be seen
With a tuneless free-verse poet.

ARTFUL POSES

White as a blown cloud face, feast of
Long hair rusty, the flaming thatch,
She flashes thin in her morning nakedness
As she steps onto a sunny trail, oblivious,
Her completeness at peace with itself.
I forget how to breathe at the presence,
As if fearing to break something fine,
A delicate instantiation of artistic tradition.
She senses me and hides behind fingers
And then slips into bushes by the trail,
Shimmering white skin and green leaf
Composed through fluorescent scrim.
She is relished, appreciated, but not ogled
In her motions of charm and shy elegance.
Something painterly resides in the vision,
Icy Renaissance skin, fin de siècle decadence,
And Mannerist fingers covering a breast,
All the poses artfully leaving me in seconds.
She speaks to elusive inspirations of paintings,
The modeling of such modesty and grace,
As though I had ever asked the question.

BETTER POEMS

A finely articulated incoherence
Presumes its own kind of recognition.
After all, what else could you say
When confronted by all new words
Of morning's stumbling oracle?
The words weave an intricate fluency,
A sculpted frame but with no picture
Other than the urgency that fills it.
"Did that man ask you for money?"
A security guard wants to know.
Some sense perhaps? That wasn't it.
No, he wanted me to reply in tongues
What cannot be spoken in our own,
To say what words cannot readily say,
And to explain what cannot be realized.
He wanted me to write better poems.

NATURAL BRIDGE

So I slip into thin grass by a turnout,
Mindful of a casino of bad luck,
Bad decisions, tight slots of fortune
That are misfortune, and, dare I say,
Dire disappointments of a personal
And grimly romantic nature.
Snaps of grasshoppers in weeds
Keep rhythms of dead time here.
Heady vistas of bourbon-stained infinity
Knock hard on the heart's carapace, but
Mind cannot reach to the vastness.
Some jackrabbit ears strain risks,
Hear scurrilous rumors of me,
A dangerous truth of hard rimrock
Cradled deep in my thoughts.

Sandstone worked by wind for eons
Assumes the shape of a single sound, O,
To become a bridge, but to what ends?
I no longer care what wind whispers
With this symbol of its persistence
Sawn into a worn and gritty sky
In the long forgetting of time.

All is zeroed out in this dry land
Except as suggestions of caprice
Caught at the corner of vision
In the direction of fading sun,
Where several women balance
Silently among tumbled boulders,
Draped in somber, flowing robes
That shade stone in gentler tones
Of deep purple approaching black.

They do not mimic but interpret
The hard rock behind the fabric.
They are entranced by last rays
Of the knot of opalescent sun
Similarly masked in thin clouds.
Ah, beautiful, serene, and mine,
The eye of a sudden inward turn.
Lines soften to a labile instinct
That watercolor might express
As colors gradually flow together
In various gradations of darkness.

PENDEJO AND BIRD

From beneath fluttering shadows
Played by a gust of dry wind that
Quakes through juniper branches,
Pendejo, spits a lone bird at me,
Remembering water that blessed
This dry landscape with some life.
It perches on the concrete fountain
That contains nothing but dryness,
And squawks angry accusations.
I could have done better, it says,
For all that was given to the wind.
From distraction and indifference,
I have let wonders slip into desolation.
Not caring prefigures another death,
A soulless world of drought.

By a dry garden pond of clutter,
In a basin of such losses as these,
We wash our disappointments
Together in hot, lifeless sand
Where once cool water splashed.

A NEW OWL

Soft calls of a hidden owl
Announce a new prospect
In the quiet woods nearby
Where once another lived.
On nights so cold air cracked,
On nights so black the heart
Went wobbly on a person,
The owl was never lonely
(That emptiness is our burden),
Only alone, unanswered,
But not unheard in stillness.
The darkness had a voice
Across deeps of the peaceful
Surface where night rippled
Liquid black under wings.
Lost hours were measured
By those gentle, soothing calls
Until dawn saved me again.
I have listened for that voice
Haunting inescapable tangles
Of endless, untamed nights
Where a new owl is needed
To soothe an unsettled mind.

A CAUTION

Where snow trims tops of adobe walls,
A small piñon fire of branches smolders
In a field where luckless men have gathered.
Winter night thickens, and you could die of it.
When the greasy bottle comes around
Bearing imprints of some quick kisses
And filled with stillborn breaths of others,
Pass it back, though liquor smells as sweet
As woodsmoke quaint with old memories.
Listen then to words, the terror of words
You hear in wind's wild returning wail,
Slashing across snowy arroyos and ridges,
Murmuring names just beyond hearing
Where something fierce is hunting souls.
You cannot so rashly drink of the story here
Because its cold can close your throat forever,
Because that movement distracting the eye
Is a figure frantically pacing on black ice
In a cloak of darkness beyond fire's reach,
Calling all her lost and broken lovers home
Through despair, pain, and disdain of life
Into the peace of her eternally cold embrace.

SIDE POCKETS

The first wet petal of dawn opens pink over there.
A back-busting truck ride follows inevitably
Down the rocky spill of a hill preaching gravity.
The worn out springs are as flat and useless
As distant memories of a once-smooth ride.
I am carrying another load of heavy darkness
To the world before the sun even knows it—
And wire, plastic bottles, and branches.

You must love that old truck,
People say who know little of love,
Less of trucks, and nothing of me.

I say, This is the truck I drive in hell.
Vexed metal wears and snaps away clean,
Hexed electronics smoke, burn, and die,
Leaving quarter-inch gaps in the journey.
Side pockets hide salvation's practical tools
Against the usual breakdowns on the road:
Screw drivers, flashlight, some pliers, tape,
Always the wrong tool for a desperate job
In a hot engine corner just beyond reach.
And a sunburned parchment scripture,
Contemporary American Poetry,
Honed against the metal and the years
For just such roadside breakdowns.

LAUGHTER, PERSISTENCE, BOURBON, AND SOME TIME

Two men appear on a ridge
With their japes and guffaws.
Ancient mules trudge ahead
And pull a rattling wagon
Along ruts in desert sand.

They come to retrieve the sun
From the west at end of day
And bring it home before dawn
Clothed in a black tarp of stars.
Clearly, they were low bidders
In the heavens' larger schemes.
They will surely arrive in time
Before the toil of mankind
Goes on too long unabated.

The grizzled old men sing
Crazy songs over weary mules
And strum their mandolins
And chuckle through stories
With long-forgotten endings.
Bottles pass hand to hand
And empties sparkle behind.
With laughter, persistence,
Bourbon, and some time,
They will surely get there
In time to end the day
And make the difference,
But that is why some days
Are longer than others.

HAPPY HOUR

In shaded patinas of late afternoon,
Tables of golfers relive the game
And bless a well-coiffed desert bar—
Scotch and soda, bourbon on the rocks.
Laughter and shouts echo in special light
That invokes the first of the evening stars.
Golf prevails beyond the river's steely glow
While ghostly imprints of a different story
Peer out from walls of hotel hallways
To signify some profound difference
Woven into the skin of their design:
Clouds are stacked like concrete blocks and
A round-faced sun stares through angry slits
As culture is rendered back as decor.

Diesel whiffs of civilization and noise
Are strange across darkening lawn
Laid upon the back of desert sand
As a truck rolls into earthly paradise
And disturbs the trance of perfection.
Where the hell are we then, we ask,
In what finely arranged madness
In the heart of the old killing fields?
What is this concoction with umbrellas?
Oh, unhappy hour! Oh, doubly unlucky man!

War bonnets of doubt ride the sunset,
Come at us from the heart once again,
Bent on whatever erasures are required,
Whatever deaths, whatever uncertainties,
And the unease that prevails at twilight.
The killing occurs beneath woven eyes,
Eyes that weep for what we are not
And not for the nature of our demise.

Phillip Brittenham ~ 95

ALL THE WORDS

Joe, the cowboy, shoed the ranch horses
In drizzling spring for "dudes" to ride.
He blew up from Antonito on black wind
Hunched in the boss's pickup, hung over,
Which was a lot like most of the time.
"Where have you been?" I asked him.
"Where I always been," he grumbled.
"Boss just never came to pick me up."
He was not street legal in any state,
But could ride horses like a son of bitch.
He did everything like a son of a bitch,
And he could dance like a whirlwind,
Freed from aches and disappointments
Where ladies called him their sweet José.
He had disappeared from the bunkhouse,
But he would return when it was time.
One night after work, back in the same old,
He told me, "This book has the words—
It has all the words, what they mean too."
"A dictionary," I replied, dismissing him
With a tin ear yet for the ways of wonders.
"No," he snarled as if he were teaching me
The way he tied a rope or forged the iron,
"I said, all the words, all the goddamn words!"

THROUGH THE WINDOW

Through a window of dream
Gradual slopes of valleys
Fluoresce with hot colors
Almost molten to the eye.
The figure representing me
Startles alert at vistas
Of impossible breadth.
He thinks, How is it that I
Have lived so long and never
Experienced this marvel?
Is it a trick of light or mind?

The figure representing me
Has suggested an awareness
That he is truly and fully alive
And possesses a subtle mind
Capable of creating illusions.
He even thinks he has a past.
This is a most disturbing level
Of self-consciousness dreamed.
Sometimes these shadowy figures
Wonder if they are in a dream,
But always decide they are not.
They seem held in the confines
Of time and place within dream,
Beyond which nothing else is real.
If this figure were fully to realize
His freedom, then the dream itself
Might become as if entirely real
To him and thus to the figure
Representing the wakening me,
Beginning our shared madness
As dream turns into memory.

Phillip Brittenham

A BOX OF CATS

Some cats are like Existentialists,
Cadging each nibble from life.
They spend nights lounging in clubs
And restaurants on Crete where
Something might come their way,
A flake of fish, a smidgen of butter,
If nothing violates their wildness,
Their well-articulated freedoms.
Aloof, indifferent, they are working
As they see the task before them,
But they are easily bribed to resemble
The idea of what cats should be.
Old couples secretly dropping treats
Are exposed by circles of cats that
They can only pretend are coincidental.
It's a living and cats seldom complain.
Cool as a cat is good practice.
Life rubs them the wrong way,
It playfully pulls at their tails,
Yet they follow it everywhere.
Some people disrespect cats.
Their problems are manifest.
Some people are like cats.
They are like Existentialists.

COMPOSITION WITH YUCCA

Choirs of yucca flowers cast
Into bells of white hanging light
Bloom amidst spears and spikes
That are the plant's hostile truth.
Each flower is achieved in its form,
Hanging from a thin central stem.
Yucca then breathes into quiet air
A syrup so neurally compromising
That notions of such fine fragrance
Rolling over words would scarcely
Reach seductions of its exhalation.
Not only bees are thus bedazzled.
Crazy lushness of this lone yucca
Vamps a field in fogs of sweetness,
Like a beautiful woman in a slow,
Deliberate dance across a vision
Synchronized with her in time
And carrying the dance floor
Of a flat field of grass and scrub
Into the centrality of her motion,
Which is the nature of composition.

BLUE NIGHTGOWNS

Women in blue nightgowns
Cross bedrooms all over America
Like automatons or sleepwalkers.
Nothing is spoken, nothing is known,
As if they are finally at peace alone.
They have forgotten what you are,
A ghostly presence in the room
That occupies your space, your loafers,
And fingers your relics to no end.
But what of God, the possibility of grace,
The short lives of insects? Death?
What can these ever mean to us?
The world aches with questions.
You are consumed in distractions.
To these women, you are already dead,
And you have been so for years—
If only you would stop talking about it.

SECOND CHANCES

Midnight in an abandoned gas station
Beneath a dusty circle of moon
On a stretch of crumbling asphalt
Where the highway turns away.
A cold intention released tonight looks
For itself as something in darkness
Until sunrise breaks its heart again.
Someone from a former life returns
To haunt a lost moment now recast
As the desolate wreckage of a mind.
Memories of urgent words long gone
Are shouted into a telephone mouthpiece
That is unplugged, broken in half-light.
The number is anyone, place nowhere.
Someone still has something left to say
With a useless mouth full of dry rot.
He spits out once again, "Jesús, come
Get me out on old Highway 666
Someplace just south of Farmington."
This is what a disordered rummage
Through various boozy memories
Is like, shafts of crazy moonlight
That touch night loss and leave
Something rattling in an empty bay.
It's coyotes and sand on the roadway.
The phone is dead, the voice off the hook.
No one breaks the silence repeated.
No one picks up on second chances.

Phillip Brittenham ~ 101

THE NEW SCHOOL

Fortifications have slumped away,
Taking too echoes of rebel yells.
The country corner is gone for good
With its plank loafing bench and shade,
And throughways replace old ways.
Rebel chic is a fashion statement
For men out of step and their trucks.
Back then, before time reconstructed us,
A lone black boy along the busy road
Across the swamp of our gnarled history
Said that he just wanted to go to school
Where the white kids went to school.
Things may get better, but they never
Get right where justice was cheated.
As much as the world can hurt you,
It is irony that hurts the most when
It twists a knife into the living heart.
Just imagine what it was back then,
The old cabins deep in the swampland,
The batons and snarling dogs punishing
The flesh for what the soul demanded,
And what it is today, the new school
He longed for, built atop his old home.

ONE NOTE

The car must have been warming
When Mrs. Miller told me to hit
That one note until she returned,
Not that there was ever any sign
That music might come from the piano.
But she never returned. It was legendary
How she and that preacher man lit out
Like a couple of criminals on the run.
Their love trapped them in a way
That was mostly of their own making.
Whether she tempted him or he her
Long remained an unsettled matter
Until eventually no one cared anyway.

I imagine her tinkling her fine ivories
In the vast Pacific Ocean after escaping
The ruin and rumor of a Southern village.
Freedom must have seemed boundless
With the water and that man before her,
For a while anyway until the stale set in.
In that moment, though, she could reply,
This belongs to me now. This is my due.
And she left a note to remember her by.

MARCH HARE

Wind soughs through barren branches,
And sky is bruised with crimson moments.
The air is possessed by heaviness of rain
As first drops furrow down windowpanes.
Then the heedless old March Hare mutters,
Let it fall, so much of winter and of spring.
Let it fall, fall with the certainty of days.
There is always time for tea in the season.
The iron patch in the center of the ceiling
Wets its eye and droops dangerously.
It testifies to chores undone, neglect,
Speaks of what was accepted then,
Sunlight weaving days together
Into garments of casual forgetting.

It is a matter of life and death, finely put.
It distills to a diamond delicately suspended
In the center of all that is owed to time
For days past and nights still to come
Unless some unwise person touches it and
Brings the whole house down upon a finger.

ROUTINE MONSTERS

By the dim light of stars
On a moonless night
When wind falls silent,
Breathless in the interval,
I recall…no, I evoke, incur,
The horror of the crime,
The nature of ordinary evil
And the routine monsters
Of the all-too-human mind
That write cruel conclusions
In the illegible hand of madness.
It was always futile and stupid,
Like most stories of the kind
Where the end goes all askew.
I wonder what others see here,
Passing this secluded turnout,
Given the shortness of memory.
I wonder if I will ever think that
Love and generosity were not faults
That delivered the victims to their fate.
My thoughts are pillaged by such truths.

SPLENDID

These women are so splendid,
With their so carefully studied
Positions of the mouth and lips,
Purple shades of noblesse, and
The bedbug pinch of new boots.
They repose in a blinding sheen.
They flatter silver and turquoise,
They make their jeans look good,
Pooching in places they should,
But there is no nakedness beneath,
Just more layers of artificiality,
The skin cut and stretched out
To a new conception of the self.

An old man sweeps into a motion
Down the sidewalk with them,
He is not the charm of the place,
With his face of worry and woe,
For he is the spirit of desolation.

Rad storms of self-involved air
Cross a desert of their making.
They hardly notice their captive
As they relentlessly shop onward:
Look, ladies, on sale there,
In that wrinkle of glass—
Glorious blue Gucci sky!

He knows they cannot see him
In this guise as he sees them,
Still wrapped in indulgence.
Yet he bestows a benediction
Because he has been alone
With each of them when some
words were said, promises made.

THE BURNING ROAD

Memories freighted with remorse and shame
Eventually return to haunt the penitent one,
Who wonders at a great crudity of feeling,
Basic failures of humanity in one's doings
So lacking in compassion, so very lacking.
Today is a small town in the path of a firestorm
Fed by guilt and regret. Nothing is contained.
Nothing is constrained in the way of feeling
Where asphalt of the road sizzles and smokes,
Where the way here, the past itself, is lit.
Air is a caustic piss yellow, and everything
Is drained of definition and meaning
As smoke mutes the colors in the eye.
Residents have all fled the danger, except
The one who will not leave, who cannot escape
The elaborate personal puzzle of the metaphor
With words and recriminations flocked to the stars.

Demons torment the self-damned persons
In the kind of hell constructed of remorse
Beyond forgiveness or balm of understanding.
But beyond forgiveness? The concept sickens.
A demon has won the trick, played death
And laid down the final card that is damnation.
So it is forever, timeless in the abandoned town,
Unless someone stirs and boldly acts instead
To clench a mindful destiny from murky air
That is a kind of hope one can breathe into.
First, though, one must wish to leave.
Second is anyone's guess.

THE CRUSHER

Boxcars rattle their loose jewelry
Beside the old road from Laguna.
Clouds briefly cover sunflowers
That later return to dazzle again,
Forming lagoons of golden color.

Hey, blondie, the old Indian slurs
Inside a bar past the reservation line.
I could be this blondie, I suppose.
He moves over to an empty stool.
At first, he is mean and threatening,
Not knowing what he wants from me.
Then he starts to talk about the crusher,
Breaking rock all night in choking dust
And every kind of racket hell can raise
Inside a pall of ghoulish light.

No good, he says through thickness of drink,
No good ever comes of the goddamned crusher,
Eating stone in darkness and shitting road base.
Feeding the crusher through the endless nights,
He broke like the hardest stone there is, he says,
And he just thought someone should know, is all,
As if there might be some kind of forgiveness.

CLOSED VILLAGE

Dancers wear faces and attitudes of animals,
Draped in sprays of evergreen and bright colors.
I am stranded again in the Indians' thankfulness
Drumming like a rain of iambics on the brain,
Like fingers on the desk of indifference. Well,
My superficiality has significant moments too,
Its own rhythms, and its own calendar to keep.

The Butterfly Dance at Hopi, the Deer Dance
at San Ildefonso, I've bumbled through them all.
In this matter of enlightenment v. entertainment,
It is hard to know the moment when either bleeds;
But bleed they finally do, and things mix together.
The complex rigmarole of precise performance
Clears its own space in mind when you get it.

The beat of the drums affirms that this thing
Is moving out. Catch onto it where you can.
Reverence in all its dawn faces and demands
Emerges like exhilaration when unity appears,
Realized through advent of an understanding
That must be recovered or recreated each time.
No, you don't get it as they get it, but it is yours.
And you can speak of it only in the closed village
That is the hidden dimension of your heart.

PINK CHIFFON

In the midst of shopping with you, alligators.
I hear their missteps in slick, blind alleys
Dangerous noplaces dark between spaces
Where glitz wears off the gilding of the day
And stealthy gators time their mortal play.

We have much to atone for in the afternoon,
But I convey no apologies for the pink chiffon.
Two seconds and we're on our way down deep.
They carry us, carrion, to their lair beneath the world
Where they primp us, eyeless, like drowned children.

Umbrellas of blue and red litter some foreign shore
Where our skins were found lacking and filled again.
The white duck asks if we'd like another of these
For myself and for the lovely lady sitting to my right,
Radiantly robed in this pink chiffon…you.

OUTER SPACE

If some being not unlike a person stares up
Through usual sky of a dreary job completed,
Perhaps involving something like a shovel,
And rubs some stardust from his hands,
He may focus on your space in the universe
Where the evening stars begin to snap on.
Perhaps you are a little anxious, harried,
And running late with evening coming on
And some time allotted for love, a thought
That carried you through just another day.
The moon has risen ripe and honey sweet
On a horizon so high above your own
That you do not even see it in your hurry,
Or the celestial corner where that being
Looks up at you through a smudge of light,
Imagining you or something much like you
With such a sense of wonder that he must
Cherish you for that moment as a part
Of the lovely glow in the distant sky
Without knowing where or what you are.

Phillip Brittenham

AUTOMATED READER

A mechanical voice startles me,
This automated poetry reader,
Pretending to gender and humanity,
And more real for it, as we also strive.
Maybe this voice insults listeners
With lack of concern for their needs,
But it is clean and metallic, perfect.
It does not care what anyone thinks
Or even care that anyone thinks.
Words pass devoid of meaning,
Which is itself a kind of insult
To poet and poem, to audience.
There is no flow of a notion,
No idea strung along verses.
Words collapse into just sounds,
Freed of passionate purpose,
As I too no longer trust
In passionate purpose.

Voice soothes defiance of lines,
Reads with unfeeling regularity of
A soulless machine, like icy fingers
Of irresistible indifference, oh!

SHOUT OUT

Shout out your order when your turn comes round.
Slap of mayo on a bun, fingers dealing ham,
Lettuce, pickles, smell of onions in yeasty air,
Laughter, coughing, cold wind at the door
When someone leaves, when someone slips in
And the whoop-whoop of the ceiling fans.
Conversations like the violent clash of spoons,
Work across hubbub: How 'bout that, she said what,
What do you know, you don't say, no kidding,
No shit, no wonder, you won't believe this but,
That's alright, that's ok, come on now, cool.
A little sugar in the coffee and a reach for the cream.
"Hand me the salt there, bud. This your first time here?
Because you look like a lost dog sitting there is all."
The plate bangs down and a bell rings a ding. "Friend,
You can have what you want, but you must shout it out."

NIGHT FISHING

Beneath a gray, disgruntled mist,
Waves engage in some rough play,
Slap hard against a night-swept pier
Hard enough to shake big timbers
Down to their roots deep in sand.
Violence overwhelms our voices
Beneath haloes of decayed light.
We say no more than we need to,
And a cold shore of isolation forms
Just beyond our gloved fingertips.
Waves blow apart, and black tongues
Of water search and sizzle through feet
Of fishermen in their heavy boots.
Diamonds are strung on fine filaments
And offered to the surging waves.
Hooks, like question marks, are baited
With feelings of perfect darkness,
But return with ordinary answers.
Dark muscles of waves flex, crash,
Gurgle, and retreat, communicate
An urgency in sudden tugs on lines.
The water is full of hidden teeth,
And the sky is wet and slick with stars,
Cold, indifferent mysteries, above as below.
Jackets are tight to wind, caps pulled down,
And coolers snapped shut, full of privacy
And our reasons for coming here tonight.
We are different while night fishing.

A CAT IN THE PARKING LOT OF TIME

A black and white cat scurries
Across an empty parking lot.
In a moment a ferry looms,
And then groaning of metal
And shouts and engine noise.
It cracks open and disgorges
Autos and trucks across the lot,
So much activity and hubbub.
I clamber onto the ramp
Into this smoky darkness
And then quickly up the stairs
Into a cabin that looks like
A parody of a sixties strip bar.
So this is the deliverance
Across the wine dark seas
That floated so many tales.
I am on a soulful journey into
The heart of ancient myth
And history where I have lived.
There will be consequences
As the cost of that experience.
What will one learn on
The other side of legend?
What will one think instead
As innocence and poetry fade?
The days then can only be
A procession of ordinary days
Cast in an ordinary light that
Is not the more refining one
Of the imagination engaged.
Does stark reality leave traces
Of the fine heroic vision or
Does one emerge with the hard

Stare of cynicism and even
Indifference for the made-up
Pandering of a blind old poet?
When I look back to shore
The parking lot is empty again,
The black and white cat returns
Across the empty parking lot
That is eternity waiting for itself
Between events that speak nothing.

PEOPLE AND POEMS

When clouds roiled gray,
Perpetually gray all day,
And the black sea bore
The dreck of disaster
Onto the oily sand,
Men hunted rats and wild
Housedogs in brick piles.
A cold and dreary feeling
Filled the hearts of all, and
Gods dared not try to atone
For such dark times as these.
Then the remaining People
Needed to find poetry again
For all that was not born,
For all that did not bloom.
A few words were banked
Against the endless gloom
To lift heavy stones again
To build the world anew.

THE MINOTAUR

Imagine, the Minotaur following here.
The soul and voice of old grievance,
Its groans are muffled from deep inside
The somewhere that holds it captive.
The heft of its shoulder shakes walls.
Alone, it is the only one of its kind,
And loneliness has driven it mad.
It is the wind of blood and wild stink.
It thrives on the sour taste of darkness.
It wanders the labyrinth of its making
Lost in fits of anger and anguish.

For what is it searching? A door?
Maybe a way out into the world.
Its head slings drool onto the walls
As it searches for entrances and exits.
Maybe it needs a way inside the way
As we need to get inside ourselves,
Some way to save itself from its journey,
Then from the journey inside the journey
That goes on and on and on, infinite.
The labyrinth is its home, our home,
With one way in and no easy way out.
Does no one love the struggling Minotaur
Enough to kill it finally with some peace?

WINDFALL PEACHES

Solitude and splendor of enfolding hills
Scarcely elevated the old community.
Newcomers noticed the predilection
Of inhabitants to endless blood feuds
Stirred with influences of drug addiction.
They learned to be sensitive to sudden
Mood swings just in the air and distant
Gunshots echoing far down the valley.
But there were artists too, who wove
Colorful designs while ancient guitars
Played faintly at night. Men still tended
To fields planted with their fine chile
Into growth cycles of hope and faith.
Kids dreamed of futures unborn and
Waited in introspection for a way away.
A rickety old man counted it providence
When windfall peaches filled his yard
From the lone surviving tree untended,
And he sold his sour fruit to tourists
As the sweetest ones they ever tasted.
Even his path was strewn lavishly with
Pink blossoms blown everywhere
In the generosity of early spring
As though he was something special.

PETROGLYPH

A rabbit chipped in sandstone
Stops the climb as someone
Long gone cries out loudly
Along the rimrock trail,
Rabbit! Seek it here.
Or perhaps it means, Rabbit!
Be like the rabbit, rapt,
Alive to land and sky,
To see the rabbit here.

Rabbit perches motionless
On a flat face of stone,
For all time if necessary,
Waiting for someone
To finally see it moving
In mind and meanings,
Even after centuries.
Rabbit is what hides
The intention expressed,
The mystery formed
Of another person
That ever escapes us
Into elusive uncertainty:
Rabbit! it shouts.

www.ingramcontent.com/pod-product-compliance
Lightning Source LLC
Chambersburg PA
CBHW011955150426
43199CB00020B/2871